PRAISE FOR
I AM WHO GOD SAYS I AM

"Gripping from the very first page. As Alicia sets the scene of stand-ing before God and He says, "You are mine" – that blew my mind away! Reading her book was like chatting with a girlfriend, Alicia was so open, transparent, vulnerable, and engaging. I hung on every word and nugget of wisdom that God imparted to her to share with us. It was like receiving water in a desert. For anyone who desires to know who God says you are in Christ Jesus, READ THIS BOOK!"

Olesia Fisher, Everyday Mom

"In *I Am Who God Says I Am*, you will discover an urging to dive into the topic of identity and come out the other side rooted in Christ. Through Biblical narrative and personal stories, Alicia guides readers to the heart of Jesus. With humor and candor, she shares His desire for us to shake off the shabby garment of false identity we find in the world and clothe our-selves in identity aligned with His truth. I wholeheartedly recommend adding this book to your must-read list!"

Jennifer Elwood, Author and Host of the Refuge Podcast

"A life-changing and powerful book! First, this book had me laughing. Second, it moved me to tears. And, finally, it challenged me to evaluate the health of my own identity. Alicia does an amazing job of teaching about identity using her own personal life stories as well as those of the Bible. I highly recommend this book to anyone who feels lost in their identity and needs hope and lasting freedom. If that's you, this book is your answer!"

Ushirika V. Johnson, LPC, Licensed Professional Counselor

"An absolute must-read! It is such an easy read. It seems the writer was actually talking to me, very conversational. Instead of watching TV to unwind at night, I pick up this book and read it. Often, I have to stop myself from staying up and reading the whole book in one sitting. I just want more, and more, and more. It has helped me to consider myself more highly than I did before. I highly recommend this book to any woman, at any stage of her life."

Octavia Norris, Founder and Executive Director, Benevolent Home Design

"The honesty and candor of this book encourages those who are embarrassed to share their experiences as they seek to find God. Often, we miss out on the opportunity to heal because we hide what we have gone through. Missing out on discovering the love and compassion of Jesus is a tragedy! It is my hope that this book will reach many who are seeking to know God and who will learn to forgive themselves."

Lucinda Rudin, Retired Teacher

"Powerful and timely for this age and generation! With many people struggling in their identity today, this book is a must read to realign ourselves with who the Almighty Heavenly Father says we are. Alicia's stories and encouraging words will bless you and change your life."

Cheryl Richter, Born Again Believer in Jesus Christ

"God tends to speak to me through repetition and while reading a different book on understanding my identity, I was given a copy of this book. I LOVED the parallel! The vulnerability it took for the writer to write these words and the clarity she received is such a powerful encouragement for women everywhere, and most assuredly me."

Elaine Lincoln, Vice President, Kindred Oaks, Lincoln Chapel, and ZuZu's Petals

"In *I Am Who God Says I Am* the author shares beautiful stories, including her own, of women who allowed the world to shape some part of their identity, and how they ultimately found freedom with Christ. These stories are a reminder that, as women, we may have different experiences, but we share so many of the same false identity issues. In each chapter, Alicia gracefully points us back to the truth of scripture and beautifully illustrates how we can find true freedom through our relationship with Christ."

Jennifer Stabler, Wife and Mom of three

"WOW...Words of Wisdom! I am amazed this is Alicia Terry's first book. She did a phenomenal job of encapsulating biblical stories with current day situations, all supported with scriptures, plus she prayed for you! It can be challenging to get to the core of one's identity; however, from cover to cover, *I Am Who God Says I Am* provides that guidance."

Ann Derrick, Career Coach and Trainer

I AM WHO
GOD
Says
I AM

But as many as received Him, to them He gave the right to become children of God...
—John 1:12 (NKJV)

I AM WHO GOD Says I AM

Getting to the heart of your identity

ALICIA TERRY

ISBN: 979-8-9880662-0-0 (paperback)
ISBN: 979-8-9880662-1-7 (ebook)

Published by Above the Fray Publishing
P.O. Box 687
Round Rock, TX 78680

Cover and Book Design by HMDpublishing

CONTENTS

DEDICATION

To my mom, Katharine Edith Terry.
I love you.

ACKNOWLEDGEMENTS

To my editor, Melanie Chitwood. I so appreciate your editing expertise in helping to make a good thing better. Your cheerleading and support when life got bumpy for me is appreciated more than you can know.

Thank you, Maggie and Whitney, for allowing me to share your stories. I have no doubt that your words will touch the hearts of many women and bring about amazing freedom and change in their lives.

Thank you to the many friends who heard me talk about this book for years and never failed to encourage me to write it and finish it. May God bless each and every one of you.

A WORD TO THE READER

For years I wanted, and tried, to write this book, but the timing was not right, and I was not ready.

I was focused way more on what I wanted to say than what God wanted to say through me. I laugh now because I never intended to put my business out in the street the way I have. The Holy Spirit hijacked my writing in the first chapter. From that point on, writing *I Am Who God Says I Am* became very personal. It was about yielding and transparency as well as discovery and restoration.

As God did a work in me, I pray, through this book, He will also do a work in you to bring you to the full knowledge of who He says you are and the freedom that comes with it.

Alicia

But as many as received Him, to them He gave the right to become children of God…
—*John 1:12 (NKJV)*

CHAPTER 1

You Are Mine

*But now thus says the L*ORD*, he who created you, O Jacob, he who formed you, O Israel: "Fear not, for I have redeemed you; I have called you by name, you are mine."*
—Isaiah 43:1 (ESV)

Imagine yourself standing before God as He looks deeply into your eyes with such love and compassion as He tells you, *"You are mine."*

In just three words God cancels out every single ounce of rejection, abandonment, or worthlessness that you or I have ever felt. Imagine that. The God of all creation makes it a point to let us know we belong to Him, that we are accepted, not rejected. We are not worthless but have great value in His eyes. And God's eyes are the only eyes that matter. Dare to look into them and receive what they so passionately express, *"I know you like no other. I formed you and called you by name. You are mine."*

Upon hearing God's words, would your heart melt with gladness or harden with resistance because being accepted, feeling worthy, or embracing your value is uncomfortable? If, like me, you're finding it hard to embrace what God says about you, I understand. To believe what God says about me sometimes is a daily struggle. Maybe it is for you too.

Over time I began to recognize how so many things—past circumstances, the words of others, cultural influences, and my own thinking—all played a role in how I defined myself. I struggled to know who I really was because I never took to heart my identity being found in God and what He says about me in His Word. Nothing else.

What about you? Have you spent time learning what God says about you in His Word? If God's Word is not defining you, telling you who you are, then who or what is? Could it be family members, co-workers, friends, or even enemies? Perhaps you've given too much credence to what is being pushed on you via television, music, social media, and the culture at large. Perhaps traumatic events or the cruel words of others have impacted you more than you care to admit.

Whatever those negative influences are, we need less of them defining us and way more of God telling us who we are. What God thinks and what He says are the only things that should carry any weight. All the voices we have whispering into our ears need to line up with what God has spoken, or we shouldn't be listening at all. Information that falsely defines our identity always creates a crisis.

Identity Crisis

Take a long hard look in the mirror and see if you know the woman looking back at you. Do you recognize her? Look beyond her facial features, the shape of her eyes, the length of her hair, or the hue of her skin. Is she a woman who has allowed her identity to be determined by past circumstances and decisions or by the Word of God?

If you're like me, somewhere along the way you lost your way. You didn't realize that certain life circumstances, the words of others, the ever-changing cultural standards, and your emotional response to them all played significant roles in defining you and even dictating your behavior. I know this firsthand because it happened to me.

The Kiss of Death

A girl's first kiss should be special. It shouldn't kill you, but that's what nearly happened to me. No, the boy didn't have poison on his lips, but it was all over his advances that I responded to. Over the years, for decades, in fact, I died more and more to my true self because of the precedent set when I was just thirteen years old. Let me tell you the story. You may be able to relate to it.

My first serious kiss should have never happened. I was ending my eighth-grade year when a popular high school guy was showing me attention, and I liked it. Problem was, he had a girlfriend, and I knew it. But there I was—so excited this guy was showing interest in me that I didn't think about his lack of integrity or mine, for that matter.

Like marijuana is considered a gateway to more detrimental drugs, that is what that kiss was to me. It opened the door to a mindset of being second. In the coming years, either I had unfaithful boyfriends or I was the "other" chic.

Needless to say, this wreaked havoc on my self-esteem. I mean, this is the kind of mess I dealt with over the years:

"A mum for some." These annoying words were repeated incessantly by a high school boyfriend during homecoming week. I think you know what "some" refers to.

"I know I don't have a right asking this, but do you have $5 I can borrow so I can get in on smoking weed with the fellas." I mean, who would ask someone this?

Or, how about the time I was driving my car and was completely caught off guard by the "disappearing act" of a guy who pulled down the seatback lever of my car so that he wouldn't be seen with me. That's a real self-esteem builder (NOT!).

Oh, I could tell you more…I think I will.

How about I go to visit a boyfriend, and he opens the door wearing the signature lipstick of a girl I know. The girl was hiding in the house. And, in case you wanted to know, the color of lipstick was Cherries in the Snow by Maybelline.

When I left home for college, I was all about school and having a good time too. The odd thing, though, is that I noticed guys with girlfriends seemed to gravitate towards me. I was new on campus, so very few people knew me. But it felt like I was sending out some type of radar signal.

I didn't think about it much at first, but after a while, I knew something else was going on. I just didn't have the spiritual maturity to know what it was at the time. Looking back, I now realize that Satan sought to destroy my identity, and worse yet, I was helping him. And it all started with that kiss.

The Words of Life

So, decades later, I find myself a single, never-before married woman in her 50s who finally is allowing God to dig deep into this soil I call my soul. I'm giving Him free reign to bury the past and resurrect the precious. And, as He did with Ezekiel in the valley of dry bones, He is commanding me to prophesy life to the identity He gave me.

Read these words from Ezekiel: "Again he said to me, 'Prophesy to these bones, and say to them, "O dry bones, hear the word of the LORD!" Thus says the Lord GOD to these bones: 'Surely I will cause breath to enter into you, and you shall live'" (37:4-5 NKJV).

So, let me check in with you right here. When was the last time you prophesied life to your identity or any aspect of your life? Are your words rooted in Scripture? Is it a daily or an occasional practice? If I can keep it real with you, my answers to those questions today are an indication of why there's been such a struggle to know myself as God intended. Could the same be true for you?

Without His Word being spoken in and over our lives and renewing our hearts and minds, it's like going into battle without a weapon. The problem with that is the enemy has a large arsenal, and he is attacking us with every weapon at his disposal to render us helpless and ineffective.

God does not desire to resurrect your identity or mine for the enemy to kill it all over again. He wants to resurrect our identities to establish us in the place of His calling for a particular purpose. Let's trust Him to get us there.

16

You Are Free

God often speaks to me through His creation—animals, pets, nature. It was a lovely day in the Spring or Summer of 2002 when God used a butterfly as His messenger. But let me give you some background first.

In my thirties, I found myself being asked to resign or be fired from a job I literally hated. The decision to leave was easy by this point. I resigned, but not before the experience of being in a toxic workplace took its toll on me. I was different. It had changed me. So much so that without knowing what I had just experienced that day, my mother sat across from me at a restaurant and kept looking at me and asking what's wrong.

I didn't tell her. Finally, she said, "Alicia, I know you're my daughter, but I'm sitting here looking at you and I don't even recognize you. You don't look like yourself." Ah, that got me. I still get emotional when I think about it all these years later. I allowed a job and the people at that job to rob me of my identity.

I was angry for a host of reasons. Somewhere between all the emotions I was feeling I fell into what I now know was depression. All I did was sleep. I literally slept through spring and had missed the flowers and trees blooming and that made me angry.

Eventually, I was tired of being cooped up in the house, so I took my dog, Rusty, for a walk. The sun felt good on my skin, and the fresh air rejuvenated me. About a block and a half into our walk, I was passing the subdivision's model home. The yard was beautifully landscaped. The flowers had bloomed and were at the height of their glory. A protective netting had been placed over the flowers to keep deer from eating them. As I admired the flowers in the bed nearest me, there was a movement that caught my eye. I saw a beautiful black butterfly trapped under the netting, looking for a way out.

I watched as the butterfly flew up as far as it could and then dropped back down—up and back down, up and back down. I lifted the netting to free it, but it didn't fly away. It just kept going up and back down as though it was still trapped. This continued until the butterfly rested in the street just off the curb. Concerned that a car might run it over, I started to pick it up to move it out of harm's way, but I had an overwhelming sense that I was to leave it there. I struggled with the decision, but I couldn't deny the overpowering veto. So, I left it there.

I continued my walk, all the while wanting to go back to rescue the butterfly. The thought of it getting run over gave me a sinking feeling in the pit of my stomach. As Rusty and I headed back to the house, I was afraid I would find the butterfly squashed in the road. When we got to the place where the butterfly had landed, it was nowhere to be found. It had, I surmised, finally realized it was free and flew off.

Relieved, I asked God what that was all about. Here's what He impressed upon my heart:

"So many of My people remain in bondage when I have already set them free. They don't realize they're free and, therefore, continue to live in their old patterns of going up and back down, up and back down. But like that butterfly, they need to pause, realize they are free, gather up their strength, and then get back to being who I created them to be."

What Do You Believe?

What God says about us and who He created us to be must become what we believe. We can be free of the old labels and lies that make us feel unworthy, unaccepted, and less than. Bill Johnson, Pastor of Bethel Church in Redding, California, said it best, "I can't afford to have a thought in my head about me that He [God] doesn't have in His head about me."

Insignificant. Worthless. Stupid. Unattractive. All lies. Yet these words and many others persistently attempt to creep into our consciousness to persuade us to believe something God never said about us.

When did God ever tell you, His creation, you are worthless? When did He ever tell you or me that no one cares about us? When did God ever say to you that you don't belong? The answer is never, but what He did say was:

"Yes, I have loved you with an everlasting love; therefore with lovingkindness I have drawn you."
(Jeremiah 31:3b NKJV)

"And it shall come to pass in the place where it was said to them, 'You are not My people,' There they shall be called sons of the living God." *(Romans 9:26 NKJV)*

"Fear not, for I have redeemed you; I have called you by your name; You are Mine." *(Isaiah 43:1b NKJV)*

It's too costly to think in opposition to God. Our very identities are linked to His thoughts of who we are. As Creator, that's His right. As His creation, it's our duty to *search* out and discover who we are in Him and who He's made us to be. Proverbs 25:2 states, "It is the glory of God to conceal a matter, but the glory of kings is to search out a matter" (NKJV).

And search it out we will, starting with Revelation 1:5-6. Look up these verses in your Bible and then answer the following question: *What did Jesus make you?*

Answer:

_____

_____

Hence, a clue to your identity. Sit with that for a moment and then ask yourself, "Is my life reflecting this identity or something totally different?"

Role vs. Identity

If I asked you, "Who are you?" Would parent, daughter, sister, employee, or wife be on your list of responses? Even though these roles are significant to us, they are not the core of our identities; they are components. Roles can come and go, but your identity is who you are if a role never existed. Make sense?

If every role, every title you've ever had ceased to exist, who would you be at the end of the day? That's what we are after with this book – knowing our real identities. It's the place where God is waiting to meet us and reveal to us the mystery of who we are in Him. God says in Jeremiah 33:3, "'Call to Me, and I will answer you, and show you great and mighty things, which you do not know'" (NKJV).

There is purpose, power, and promise in who God says we are and who He created us to be. And Satan knows it. But the question is, do we know it?

A Thief in the Garden

Satan has interfered in humanity's relationship with God ever since Adam and Eve in the Garden. Have you ever asked yourself why?

Because of his interference, God said to Satan, "'And I will put enmity between you and the woman, and between your seed and her Seed; He shall bruise your head, and you shall bruise His heel'" (Genesis 3:15 NKJV).

Enmity is a strong word. It speaks of aggressive hostility between enemies. Merriam-Webster online explains it this way:

Enmity and its synonyms "hostility," *animosity,* and *animus* all indicate deep-seated dislike or ill will. *Enmity* (which derives from an Anglo-French word meaning "enemy") suggests true hatred, either overt or concealed. *Hostility* implies strong, open enmity that shows itself in attacks or aggression. *Animosity* carries the sense of anger, vindictiveness, and sometimes the desire to destroy what one hates. *Animus* is generally less violent than *animosity,* but definitely conveys active prejudice or ill will.[1]

Satan fights dirty. He uses the actions and words of others, our life experiences, and even our own thoughts against us. If he had his way, he would have us live out our days trapped in a prison of hurt, anger, pain, bitterness, sadness, insecurity, shame, loneliness, and who knows what else. But that never was and never will be God's plan for us.

God desires us to know Him and ourselves intimately. To do so requires letting go of old, erroneous thinking to grasp for new, liberating beliefs. It's like taking on the mindset of trapeze artists who have faith to know when one lets go, the other is there to catch them. For us, that someone is God.

He is right there with His arms outstretched, ready to catch us and allow us to see Him and ourselves from a totally new perspective—His perspective.

I'm not saying it's easy because it's not. It takes time to change your mindset but change it we must if we want to live freely in the place, space, and identity God intended for us. Dare to defy the devil and, where necessary, your own thinking to become the woman God says you are.

I Am Who God Says I Am will help you:

- See how the love of a righteous King is not moved by your imperfections but by His desire to bless and restore you completely.

- Let go of the negative names and labels you've been branded with to allow the true Master of the name game to define you.

- Recognize and overcome Satan's use of lies, difficult experiences, and cultural norms in his attempt to get you to relinquish your identity and forfeit your destiny.

- Understand what role Jesus plays in revealing your identity and what that entitles you to.

Before we head into the next chapter, I just want to say how glad I am that we are on this journey together. Your reading this book tells me that you are a truth seeker and fighter. You're summoning up the courage to ask yourself, and even more important, to ask God who you are and to search for the answers, wherever they may take you. You haven't given up on yourself, and neither has God.

Throughout this book, my intention is to allow God to show us how Satan punches and how we are to counterpunch and come away victorious. Yes ma'am, my sister, we are born into battle and equipped to win wars. God will teach us how to fight like Jesus and keep our identities intact. God will do it. Do you believe?

Father,

Bless the woman who is holding this book right now. Cause her to know and understand who You created her to be and who she is in You. Let every negative word, thought, and action fall off her right now and set her heart, mind, body, soul, and spirit free. Wherever and however her identity has been usurped by the enemy, together we agree with heaven that Your original plans for her overrules, prevails, and cancels out any and all plans that are in opposition to Yours.

Now, Father, if my sister is not saved and she wants to be, may she repeat these words in prayer to You.

Dear God,

I want to be saved. I want to be Your daughter and a co-heir with Christ. I believe Jesus is Your Son who came from heaven to die for my sins, was raised from the dead, and now sits at your right hand in heaven. I admit I am a sinner, and I ask for Your forgiveness. I turn from my sins and invite Jesus to come into my heart and life right now.

In Jesus' name I pray. Amen.

Name:

_____

_____

Date:

_____

_____

If you prayed the prayer of salvation, it's important to find a Bible-believing church or group of people who you can learn from and grow with. Do your best to read your Bible regularly. I suggest starting with the Book of John in the New Testament and the Psalms in the Old Testament.

CHAPTER 2

Not Forgotten

Now David said, "Is there still anyone who is left of the house of Saul, that I may show him kindness for Jonathan's sake?" ...And Ziba said to the king, "There is still a son of Jonathan who is lame in his feet."
—2 Samuel 9:1, 3b (NKJV)

No five-year-old should have to flee for his or her life, but that's exactly what happened to Mephibosheth when word came that his father Jonathan and his grandfather King Saul had been killed in battle. His caretaker feared the Philistine soldiers would come to kill him too, so she quickly gathered him up and fled to a place called Lo Debar. By definition Lo Debar means *no pasture, without a place to feed.*[1] In other words, it's a barren land that is unable to sustain life.

So in their haste to get away, the unexpected happened. Mephibosheth took a serious fall that left him lame for the rest of his life. Lame became the name that people identified with Mephibosheth.

I'd like for you to read 2 Samuel 4:4 and pay close attention to how and when Mephibosheth is first introduced in this passage:

Jonathan, Saul's son, had a son who was lame in his feet. He was five years old when the news about Saul and Jonathan came from Jezreel; and his nurse took him up and fled. And it happened, as she made haste to flee, that he fell and became lame. His name was Mephibosheth. (NKJV)

Did you catch it? Before we know Mephibosheth by name, we come to know him by his condition — *lame*. And that name didn't disappear when he got older. It followed him into adulthood. We know this because 2 Samuel 9:12 tells us Mephibosheth was old enough to have a young son, and, just one verse later, the chapter ends with the writer letting us know, yet again, that Mephibosheth was lame in both his feet. Not to mention in 2 Samuel 9:1, when King David inquired if there was anyone left in Saul's house he could show kindness to, Ziba, a servant of Saul's, said, "There is still a son of Jonathan who is lame in his feet." I mean, come on! Stop talking about the man's feet. He is not his feet. He is Mephibosheth.

As we see, Mephibosheth became known by what happened to him as opposed to who he really was, the son of a prince and the grandson of a king. He was royalty, but in the eyes of some, he was what his fallen state had made him — lame.

Fallen and Broken, but Not Forgotten

What about you? Have you ever, in some form or fashion, experienced a fall that left you with a name that accurately represented the situation, but did not accurately reflect who you are?

The truth is falls come in different shapes, sizes, and circumstances. For my friend Maggie it came in the whispered words of a sibling when she was just a little girl.

Maggie was about seven years old when her father introduced her and her siblings to a new friend of his. He introduced them all by name, but when he got to Maggie he pointed to her and said, "That's the one that looks like me." Upon hearing it, one of her sisters leaned over and whispered in her ear, "You're ugly. You look like a man."

Nothing could be further from the truth. Maggie is a beautiful woman, inside and out, but those words kept telling her, even many years later, that she was not. And that's how Satan works. He will seize any opportunity to keep us from knowing the truth about who we are.

Proverbs 23:7 says, "For as he thinks in his heart, so is he" (NKJV). In other words, what we think about, we become. God fashioned Maggie to be a bold warrior for His Kingdom. If she's not leading souls to Christ, she's planting seeds so they can be. But for many years those words, "You're ugly. You look like a man," left her crippled in spirit to the point she would not look at herself in the mirror and felt uncomfortable being seen in public. Thankfully, that didn't remain Maggie's story. God intervened in the most amazing way to let Maggie know exactly how He saw her and how she should see herself.

While attending a women's conference, the speaker asked the attendees to close their eyes and ask God who they needed to forgive. Maggie had suppressed that memory from her childhood, but it was still impacting her life nonetheless. So she closed her eyes...why don't I let her tell the story.

I close my eyes, and I ask God, "Who do I need to forgive?" I had forgotten about the seven-year-old girl — the situation. I don't think about it all the time, but it's there buried deep down inside of me. God brings it up to the surface for me to deal with.

I see the vision of us on the couch and my sister leaning over and telling me I'm ugly because I look like a man. So, I tell God that I forgive my sister for breaking my spirit that day. She didn't know what she was doing.

So, I'm sitting there and I start to wonder, "Oh my God, am I ugly? I don't think I'm ugly." I get up and go to the restroom to look at myself in the mirror for the first time in years, and I don't see ugly. I see Maggie, and she is not ugly. She's a pretty girl. And I start to fall in love with her.

I just stand there with tears streaming down my face. I turn around and there's a woman standing there and she hugs me and says, "God says you are beautiful." I ask her how she knows what I am thinking? She says, "God told me to come and tell you that you are beautiful and He sees you beautiful."

Wow! What an awesome God that He would do that for Maggie. And you know what? He wants to do the same for you too. Wherever and however you have fallen, God is waiting and ready to restore you to His original design and wipe away the false identity that Satan would have you believe about yourself. God desires for you to know the truth and to be made whole because of it. Are you willing?

What a Righteous King Does

So remember, Mephibosheth was taken to Lo Debar (a place of no pasture, without a place to feed) by his nurse when he was a child. This is where Mephibosheth lived until he was an adult. That is until the king called him out of that barren place and into the palace.

We pick up the story at 2 Samuel 9:4 after Ziba tells King David that Mephibosheth is alive.

So the king said to him, "Where is he?" And Ziba said to the king, "Indeed he is in the house of Machir the son of Ammiel, in Lo Debar."

Then King David sent and brought him out of the house of Machir the son of Ammiel, from Lo Debar.

Now when Mephibosheth the son of Jonathan, the son of Saul, had come to David, he fell on his face and prostrated himself. Then David said, "Mephibosheth?"

And he answered, "Here is your servant!"

So David said to him, "Do not fear, for I will surely show you kindness for Jonathan your father's sake, and will restore to you all the land of Saul your grandfather; and you shall eat bread at my table continually."

Then he bowed himself, and said, "What is your servant, that you should look upon such a dead dog as I?"

And the king called to Ziba, Saul's servant, and said to him, "I have given to your master's son all that belonged to Saul and to all his house. You therefore, and your sons and your servants, shall work the land for him, and you shall bring in the harvest, that your master's son may have food to eat. But

Mephibosheth your master's son shall eat bread at my table always." Now Ziba had fifteen sons and twenty servants.

Then Ziba said to the king, "According to all that my lord the king has commanded his servant, so will your servant do."

"As for Mephibosheth," said the king, "he shall eat at my table like one of the king's sons."

Mephibosheth had a young son whose name was Micha. And all who dwelt in the house of Ziba were servants of Mephibosheth.

So Mephibosheth dwelt in Jerusalem, for he ate continually at the king's table. And he was lame in both his feet. (NKJV)

This is such a powerful account of God demonstrating, through King David, how He desires to:

- Search for us when we have fallen and hidden ourselves,

- Call us out of dead and barren places,

- Restore to us all we have lost,

- Bless us, as one of His children, with a seat at His table, and

- Love and acknowledge us despite the reason or condition of our lameness.

Mind blown! How amazing and beautiful is that? These are the kinds of truths that Satan is trying to keep us from knowing. God's Word tells us who we are and what He has given us. It's meant to empower us to live intentionally for Him despite our slip ups and falls. If we have to hobble, limp, or roll to do it, then so be it because it's not about what people see in you, but what God sees. "For the LORD does not see as man sees; for man looks at the outward appearance, but the LORD looks at the heart" (1 Samuel 16:7b NKJV).

And guess what? Lame has nothing to do with it.

Do You Want to Be Made Well?

There's always a purpose for any question Jesus asks. He once asked a man who'd been crippled for thirty-eight years a question. Jesus came upon him at the pool of Bethesda, a place where the sick, blind, and lame came in hopes to be healed by being the first in the pool when it was stirred by an angel (John 5:4).

It's interesting to note that Bethesda means *"Place of Outpouring"*[2] or *"House of Grace."*[2] I can't think of a more fitting place for Jesus to show up and perform a miracle. Here's what happened:

When Jesus saw him lying there, and knew that he already had been in that condition a long time, He said to him, **"Do you want to be made well?"**

The sick man answered Him, "Sir, I have no man to put me into the pool when the water is stirred up; but while I am coming, another steps down before me."

Jesus said to him, **"Rise, take up your bed and walk."**

And immediately the man was made well, took up his bed, and walked. (John 5:6-8 NKJV)

If Jesus poured out His grace on the crippled man to make him whole, will He not do the same for you and me? Absolutely He will! Hebrews 4:16 says, "Let us then approach

God's throne of grace with confidence, so that we may receive mercy and find grace to help us in our time of need" *(NIV)*.

It is in the place called grace that we see Jesus pouring out healing on the lame man and in so doing demonstrating His willingness to:

- Meet us where we are regardless of our condition,

- Ask the right question to stir up our faith and desire to be made whole, and

- Heal us, straighten up our walk, and set us free!

You Are Worthy to Receive the King's Kindness

Being daughters of the King makes us members of the royal family, even if, like Mephibosheth, we are hiding in the desolate place of our own personal Lo Debar. It takes a just King, an honorable and righteous King to ask, "Is there still someone among the royal family that I can show kindness to for my Son's sake...for My sake?"

Yes, someone may tell the King you are living *below the bar* in Lo Debar and that some experience has left you lame in some way, even to the point you no longer recognize or acknowledge your true identity. It may even cross your mind to speak negatively of yourself like Mephibosheth did before King David when he said, "What is your servant, that you should look upon such a dead dog as I?" But, in spite of all the identity-robbing experiences we've endured, God's heart is to bless and restore us.

Here's a powerful truth: You are worthy to receive the King's kindness because the King makes you worthy. The days, months, years we've spent fighting the battle in our hearts and the logic in our heads make it tough some days. But, to repeat what I said in Chapter 1, "We are born into battle and equipped to win wars." So what do we do about it? "We demolish arguments and every pretension that sets itself up against the knowledge of God, and we take captive every thought to make it obedient to Christ" (2 Corinthians 10:5 NIV).

God calls you by name. He says, "You are mine." He desires to show you kindness and deems you worthy of it. Isn't it time that we accept God's view of us and begin to live our lives from this new perspective? I think so. What about you?

Before we move to the next chapter, I'd like for you to write in the space below your top three takeaways from this chapter and then use the remaining space to journal your thoughts on why these three areas stood out for you.

1 _____
_____
_____

2 _____
_____
_____

3 _____
_____
_____

My Thoughts

_____
_____
_____

_____

_____

_____

_____

_____

_____

_____

_____

_____

_____

_____

_____

_____

_____

_____

_____

_____

_____

_____

_____

_____

_____

Father,

Bless your daughter and cause her to realize she's not forgotten, but, in fact, is pursued by You. If she experienced any
type of setback or trauma at any point in her life that crip-

pled her spirit and caused her to live life wounded, lame, or hidden, I ask that You show her daily, beginning today, that she no longer needs to hide. She can come out of the shadows to be exactly who You created her to be. Her identity is not tied to a fall, but to a God who is faithful and we praise You for this.

In Jesus' name. Amen.

CHAPTER 3
The Power of a Name

And so it was, as her soul was departing (for she died), that she called his name Ben-Oni; but his father called him Benjamin.
—Genesis 35:18 (NKJV)

The time of delivery had come. So, she pushed. She pushed with everything she had anticipating that she would soon hold her child in her arms. As the contractions intensified so did the pain. Nevertheless, she pushed to bring forth new life into the world. But something was different about this delivery. This was hard labor, and it was killing her.

Yet, Rachel, the cherished mother of Joseph and beloved wife of Jacob, pushed to bring forth the life of her child at the expense of her own. Rachel bore a son. And as she lay there weak and dying, she named him, Ben-Oni, son of my sorrow.

The Father Speaks

Jacob knew the importance of a name probably better than anyone else, and although he loved Rachel, there was no way he was going to let his son be called Ben-Oni. Son of my sorrow was not going to be the declaration his son would hear every time his name was called.

Jacob changed his son's name to Benjamin, son of my right hand. In other words, Jacob was saying, "You are not, nor is it in my will for you to ever become the son of my sorrow. That is not who I've destined you to be. You are the son of my right hand. You are the son of my strength, my honor, my authority." Jacob gave a better name to his child when he declared his name to be Benjamin.

A moment ago I mentioned Jacob knew the importance of a name probably better than anyone else, but I didn't explain why. Jacob had a name change too. However, his new name was not given by his earthly father, but by God. Let me give you the back story.

As a twin, Esau was born before Jacob placing him in the position to receive the first-born's blessing from Isaac, their father. But something interesting happened when Jacob was delivered. His hand grabbed ahold of Esau's heel, and because of this, his parents named him Jacob. One of the meanings for the name Jacob is supplanter. To be a supplanter is to be a person who takes the place of another through scheming, usurping, or deceit. Does this describe Jacob? Well, let's see:

- Seeing Esau famished, Jacob did not give him anything to eat until he agreed to forfeit his birthright in exchange for food.

- Jacob took advantage of his father's failing eyesight by dressing up as Esau so the first-born's blessing would be spoken over him.

- Jacob lied to his father when asked if he was really Esau.

Everything Jacob's name said he would become, he became. That is until he had a one-on-one encounter with the Living God and was given a new name – *Israel*. Genesis 32:24-29 gives the account:

Then Jacob was left alone; and a Man wrestled with him until the breaking of day. Now when He saw that He did not prevail against him, He touched the socket of his hip; and the socket of Jacob's hip was out of joint as He wrestled with him. And He said, "Let Me go, for the day breaks."

But he said, "I will not let You go unless You bless me!"

So He said to him, "What is your name?"

He said, "Jacob."

And He said, "Your name shall no longer be called Jacob, but Israel; for you have struggled with God and with men, and have prevailed."

Then Jacob asked, saying, "Tell me Your name, I pray."

And He said, "Why is it that you ask about My name?" And He blessed him there.

God changed Jacob's name to Israel because he struggled not only with men, but with God and triumphed or prevailed. Just for the record, I don't believe the Scripture passage is saying Jacob beat God, but rather he struggled with God and endured until he got what he desired – the Father's blessing.

As Jacob, he stole the father's blessing. As Israel, it was granted to him by God. And though today he is still often referred to as Jacob, it was by the name God gave him that his life was radically blessed.

What the Jacob/Israel story teaches us is that it's not how we start that matters, but how we finish. It was when Jacob encountered God and wrestled with Him that his name and nature were changed. Jacob became Israel, setting him on a path to discover who God always intended him to be as a man and ultimately a nation that prevailed with God.

His Name is Timmie

Though certainly not on the level of Benjamin and Jacob, the story of Timmie, my little Terrier dog, can teach us the power of a name, but, more importantly, the power of the Father's love.

Back in 2006, I found myself at a bed-n-breakfast some 80+ miles west of San Antonio, Texas. A co-worker and I were in the area to deliver employee training. The evening we arrived a small, flea-ridden, hungry, thirsty, little cinnamon-colored Terrier dog showed up. He had scars, a slight hind-leg limp, and eyes that would indicate allergies or a possible infection. And with all that, what I saw was a beautiful soul that needed rescuing.

Without giving you the dramatic, emotional details of the story (maybe some other time), I made the decision to bring him back with me to see if I could find him a home. Turns out the home was mine.

At one point I'd considered naming him Gimpy because of his limp (Sort of reminds you of Mephibosheth, right?). But, for some reason, that didn't sit well with me. I actually lost my peace when I considered it. I wanted to love him, not diminish him. And I didn't want to use a name that labeled him as imperfect. Perhaps somewhere in the back of my mind Proverbs 18:21 had risen up in my spirit, "Death and life are in the power of the tongue, and those who love it will eat its fruit."

Cursing someone, even a dog, was not the fruit I wanted to bear. So, I named him Timmie after a spunky ventriloquist dummy that appeared on one of my favorite episodes of the TV program *Everybody Loves Raymond*. It was his fearlessness, humor, and sassy personality that I identified with Mr. Tim, as I sometimes called him.

No, Mr. Tim was no dummy, and he was not gimpy by any means. He was not the damaged outcome of the trauma that he had experienced sometime earlier in his life. He was a living, breathing creation of God, full of love and worthy of it. To have named him Gimpy would have been like giving both him and me a taste of bad fruit each time I would have called his name. I have no clue what his name or history was before I rescued him, and it doesn't matter. His name was and always will be Timmie. No labels. No limitations. Just love.

Oh, how I loved that dog. I loved when he'd sit in my lap, turn, and look up at me with eyes of love and gratitude. I knew each time he did he was saying, "I love you. Thank you for saving me." And in return I would tell him, "I love you too." Nothing more needed to be said.

That's how it is with the Father. Though we may have strayed and have scars that would cause others to reject us, not so with God. He saves and delivers to the utmost. Why? Because He loved us from the beginning. Even before we were being formed in our mothers' wombs.

"Before I formed you in the womb I knew you; Before you were born I sanctified you; I ordained you a prophet to the nations'" (Jeremiah 1:5 NKJV).

God knows exactly the women He created us to be. It's not a secret to Him. He longs to see us search out, discover, and live according to His divine design, and that requires a life reset.

Divine Reset

As it was with Israel (the man), so it can be with us too. A single encounter with God can launch your life on a new and most amazing journey – one that reveals how God sees you, what He thinks about you, His plans for your life, and *who you are because of His Son*. Second Corinthians 5:17-19 backs this up. The verses shared below are in three different Bible translations. I've done this because I believe the different wording may help you pull out the profound richness of what it means to be in Christ.

Therefore if anyone is in Christ [that is, grafted in, joined to Him by faith in Him as Savior], he is a new creature [reborn and renewed by the Holy Spirit]; the old things [the previous moral and spiritual condition] have passed away. Behold, new things have come [because spiritual awakening brings a new life]. But all these things are from God, who reconciled us to Himself through Christ [making us acceptable to Him] and gave us the ministry of reconciliation [so that by our example we might bring others to Him], that is, that God was in Christ reconciling the world to Himself, not counting people's sins against them [but canceling them]. And He has committed to us the message of reconciliation [that is, restoration to favor with God]. (AMP)

Therefore, if anyone is in Christ, he is a new creation; old things have passed away; behold, all things have become new. Now all things are of God, who has reconciled us to Himself through Jesus Christ, and has given us the ministry of reconciliation, that is, that God was in Christ reconciling the world to Himself, not imputing their trespasses to them, and has committed to us the word of reconciliation. (NKJV)

Now, if anyone is enfolded into Christ, he has become an entirely new creation. All that is related to the old order has vanished. Behold, everything is fresh and new. And God has made all things new, and reconciled us to himself, and given us the ministry of reconciling others to God. In other words, it was through the Anointed One that God was shepherding the world, not even keeping records of their transgressions, and he has entrusted to us the ministry of opening the door of reconciliation to God. (TPT)

This is the Father and Son at work, reconciling us to our rightful place and position as children of God. They have done all the work, but it is up to us to receive it.

Now, if you're asking what all this has to do with identity, my answer is, *everything*. Becoming a child of God is a reset to the original Manufacturer's design to be and operate in the precise purpose for which the Creator intended. This is who you are. This is your identity.

And if you're willing to go further with me, let me share a few more Scriptures on what becoming a child of God entitles you to.

For God so loved the world that He gave His only begotten Son, that whoever believes in Him should not perish but have everlasting life. For God did not send His Son into the world to condemn the world, but that the world through Him might be saved. (John 3:16-17 NKJV)

If we confess our sins, He is faithful and just to forgive us our sins and to cleanse us from all unrighteousness. (1 John 1:9 NKJV)

As far as the east is from the west, so far has He removed our transgressions from us. (Psalms 103:12 NKJV)

"I will show loving-kindness to them and forgive their sins. I will remember their sins no more." (Hebrews 8:12 NLV)

Don't breeze past the Scriptures above. They unlock truths that will change your life and eternal destiny. What are these truths?

- A negative past doesn't have to influence your future.

- With Christ everything about you can be made new.

- You can be cleansed from all your sins and unrighteousness.

- God will not only remove your sins, but He will also forget them.

- God offered Jesus as a ransom for you, and Jesus willingly laid down His life so you could be reconciled and restored back to the Father as His child.

That's good news! And, if you have not yet received Jesus as your personal Lord and Savior, making you a child of God, you're invited to do so right now if you like. Read the prayer below out loud.

Father,

*You said in Isaiah 1:18, "Come now, let us settle the matter,"
says the Lord. "Though your sins are like scarlet, they shall be as
white as snow; though they are red as crimson, they shall be like
wool." You know everything about me, Father. I am a sinner,
and I am in need of a Savior, your Son, Jesus Christ. I believe
Jesus died for my sins, three days later He rose to life again, and is
seated at Your right hand with all power and authority. Today, I
choose to make Him my Lord and Savior. I repent of my sins and
ask that You remove them from me as far as the east is from the
west. Remember my sins no more. I believe You have forgiven me
and made me whiter than snow. Today I am a new creation. I
am Your daughter because of what You and Jesus have done, and
I thank You for it.*

In Jesus' name – Amen.

Welcome to the family of God! You are now a Christian
and a restored daughter of God. Now, I encourage you to do
five things:

1. Write the date of when you said the above prayer and
   accepted Jesus into your life. _____
   _____

2. Tell someone that you made Jesus the Lord of your life.

3. Read and study the Bible (Psalms in the Old Testament
   and John in the New Testament are good places to start).

4. Strengthen your relationship with God through prayer
   and/or prayer journaling.

5. Fellowship and grow with other Bible-centered believ-
   ers (church, Bible studies, etc.).

Whether your life has been challenging, smooth sailing, or sin-ridden, trust God to heal and forgive your past. Allow Him, through Jesus, to make all things new.

Can't Forget about Benjamin

As for Benjamin, he didn't grow up to become a man of sorrow or sadness. He became the leader of the tribe of Benjamin that brought forth Saul, the first king of Israel, and Paul (formerly Saul) the apostle who was transformed from being a persecutor of Christians to a man who mightily preached the gospel of Christ and wrote the majority of the New Testament.

The story of Benjamin shows us that uncertain starts or bad beginnings do not relegate us to lives of pain and sorrow. The Father is for us, and He is more than able to establish us as His daughters to be and fulfill exactly what He predestined for us.

To Be Fully Known

Of course, you know my name is Alicia, but there are some who know me well enough to call me Lee. With most family members and friends I attended school with, this is the name they know me by. However, if someone I didn't know well called me by my nickname or if I was introduced as Lee to someone I didn't know, then almost certainly I would correct them and state my name is Alicia. Why? Because a certain degree of intimacy and trust had not yet been established. To call me Lee means you know me.

On the other hand, my book editor, Melanie Chitwood, dealt with the drawbacks of people not knowing her name at times. I'm sure it was not intentional on the part of others, since she is an identical twin; nonetheless, when it happened it left its sting. Melanie recounts the experience:

In my life as an identical twin, some people called me twin when they couldn't distinguish between me and my sister. Or they'd call me the wrong name, mistaking me for my sister. I remember how much this rubbed me the wrong way, even at a young age. I wanted to be seen as - me! I wanted to be seen, known, and embraced, not as an interchangeable person but as someone unique and different from my twin.

Although our circumstances are different, both Melanie and I desired the same thing: to be seen and appropriately acknowledged for who we are. Isn't that what we all want? But even at that, as much as we think we know ourselves, do we really? Only El Roi, meaning the God who sees me, really knows. On our best day, who we believe ourselves to be pales in comparison to who God named and created us to be. Look what 1 Corinthians says about it.

For now [in this time of imperfection] we see in a mirror dimly [a blurred reflection, a riddle, an enigma], but then [when the time of perfection comes we will see reality] face to face. Now I know in part [just in fragments], but then I will know fully, just as I have been fully known [by God]. (1 Corinthians 13:12 AMP)

There will come a day when our name and our nature will be perfected, and the bits and pieces we've learned about ourselves will be fully revealed and made clear according to God's intent and purposes.

New Name. True Name.

It was the late summer or early fall of 2022 when my brother called me up to say, "I'm Rodney Terry." I responded with a hesitant and suspect, "Yeah, okay," because I thought he was attempting to set up a corny joke. He repeated the words again, "I'm Rodney Terry," and like a lightbulb cutting on, I got it. My brother and I have different fathers, and after a year of lawyer meetings and court proceedings, his last name was officially and legally changed to Terry. The reason I didn't catch what he was saying was because to me he's always been Rodney Terry despite what is said on his birth certificate.

He changed his last name to the name of the father who raised and cared for him. With that name change came greater freedom. No more third-degree because the name on his driver's license is different from what's on another document. No more fear that he would be denied the right to board a plane, which nearly happened when checking in for a flight to attend our uncle's funeral.

Are you getting the gist of why I shared this story? I want you to know that when you choose to take on the Father's name and become His child, you come under His covering and Lordship. You're no longer slave to the world's system, but you are now entitled to the freedom, blessings, and privileges of His name. And just like Jacob had a new name for his son Benjamin, God has a new name for us, and in Revelation 2:17, Jesus tells us about it.

"He who has an ear, let him hear what the Spirit says to the churches. To him who overcomes I will give some of the hidden manna to eat. And **I will give him a white stone, and on the stone a new name** written which no one knows except him who receives it.'" (Revelation 2: 17 NKJV)

That's right. One day our identities as daughters of God will align with our true names that await us in heaven, and we will become completely whole as God intended.

Texas Pastor Jimmy Evans expounds on this in his online *The Overcoming Life* series when he states, "Part of the blessing of heaven is you finally get to know your real name. Your name right now is not your real name. It's your human name. But when you get to heaven you get your real name. Part of the curse of hell is you never knew your name. You never knew who you were."[1]

Stolen Identity: Out for Your Name, Culture, Heritage

Before we head over to the next chapter, I want to share one more story with you to further emphasize the power of your identity, including your name, culture, and heritage. It's found in the book of Daniel.

Then the king instructed Ashpenaz, the master of his eunuchs, to bring some of the children of Israel and some of the king's descendants and some of the nobles, young men in whom there was no blemish, but good-looking, gifted in all wisdom, possessing knowledge and quick to understand, who had ability to serve in the king's palace, and whom they might teach the language and literature of the Chaldeans. And the king appointed for them a daily provision of the king's delicacies and of the wine which he drank, and three years of training for them, so that at the end of that time they might serve before the king. Now from among those of the sons of Judah were Daniel, Hananiah, Mishael, and Azariah. **To them the chief of the eunuchs gave names: he gave Daniel the name Belteshazzar; to Hananiah, Shadrach; to Mishael, Meshach; and to Azariah, Abed-Nego.** (Daniel 1:3-7 NKJV)

If you want to change a people, you set out to change their culture. It seems like the Chaldean/Babylonian king, Nebuchadnezzar, knew this. Why else would one seek to control what a person ate, drank, the language they spoke, the literature they read, and the name given to someone at birth?

If you want to destroy a culture, you destroy its people, and that includes their ability to reproduce. Daniel and the other young men were put in the care of the master eunuch. This would indicate a strong possibility they were made eunuchs (men who were castrated) as well. Though they weren't killed, their heritage was. But unfortunately, this is not something that happened only prior to Christ being born. We still see this happening in our society today. King Solomon once said, "What has been will be again, what has been done will be done again; there is nothing new under the sun" (Ecclesiastes 1:9 NIV).

In Psalm 127:3, King Solomon also said, "Behold, children are a heritage from the LORD. The fruit of the womb is a reward" (NKJV). But there is no such reward for a eunuch, for it's like a type of genocide. Becoming a eunuch went against God's commandment to Adam and Eve in the Garden, and that was to "'be fruitful and multiply'" (Genesis 1:28a NKJV).

It's no secret Satan desires to make us spiritual eunuchs. In the next chapter we'll look at several ways he attempts to make us ineffective people, void of any power or purpose. And, we'll discover how to recognize and overcome his deception the way Jesus did.

CHAPTER 4

But Who Are You?

And the evil spirit answered and said, "Jesus I know, and Paul I know; but who are you?"
—Acts 19:15 (NKJV)

W*ho are you?* It's a simple question, but it can be a challenging one to answer. Not everyone knows in their heart of hearts who they are. Apart from God, I can definitively say no one knows who they are, although they may think they do. To paraphrase something shared in the first chapter, *At the core of who we are, our identities, we are not the various roles we play. It's only when the roles are removed that we get to the essence of who we are—who God made us to be.*

Who are you? Along with being a challenging question to answer, it can be an intimidating question as well, especially if you don't know the answer. And if you don't know right now, that's okay. The good news is that God lays it out for us in His Word, which means it's vitally important that we read and study the Bible. Personally, coming into the knowledge of knowing who God says I am was not as complicated as I originally made it out to be. In fact, it's really simple, which we will discover in the next chapter.

But what is it about human nature that drives us at times to make things more complicated than they really are? I don't know. Maybe it's just me or maybe you are like me, trying to figure out how everything is supposed to fit together and work. But God is not asking us to figure it out. He is asking us to trust and believe His Word.

Over and over again in Scripture we are commanded to trust God: "Trust in the LORD with all your heart, and lean not on your own understanding; In all your ways acknowledge Him, And He shall direct your paths" (Proverbs 3:5-6 NKJV).

That's a life Scripture to hold onto as we sojourn through this chapter because our focus shifts more from learning about our identities to protecting them. We are now moving into the enemy's territory where we'll see how he uses deception, doubt, and a play on words in an attempt to move people off God's path onto his. We are going to study our enemy and learn how he operates. So, suit up. We are going on a reconnaissance mission.

To Know My Enemy

In the movie, *The Last Samurai*, Captain Algren (Tom Cruise) and Katsumoto (Ken Watanabe) find themselves at war with one another. Katsumoto wants to converse with Captain Algren, a captured prisoner, but Captain Algren is not in the mood for talking. Finally, the frustrated captain asks, "What do you want?"

Katsumoto replies, *"To know my enemy."*

For us, looking to see what Scripture says about our enemy is where we start. Jesus says this of Satan: "He was a murderer from the beginning, not holding to the truth, for there is no truth in him. When he lies, he speaks his native language, for he is a liar and the father of lies" (John 8:44b NIV).

Not only is Satan the father of lies, but he is also slippery enough to get us to lie to ourselves. This is why it's important to be a tree rooted in God's Word and not in Satan's soil. Fruit nourished in foul soil is not the harvest you want to reap — a harvest the seven sons of Sceva know very well.

The Danger of Self-Deception

In Acts 19:11 we learn God was working through Paul the apostle to perform extraordinary miracles of healing and spiritual deliverance. Paul, a follower of Jesus Christ, was given power and authority to perform these miracles. There were some who attempted to do the same thing but had a very different outcome.

Then some of the itinerant [traveling] Jewish exorcists took it upon themselves to call the name of the Lord Jesus over those who had evil spirits, saying, **"We exorcise you by the Jesus whom Paul preaches."** Also, there were seven sons of Sceva, a Jewish chief priest, who did so.

And the evil spirit answered and said, **"Jesus I know, and Paul I know; but who are you?"**

Then the man in whom the evil spirit was leaped on them, overpowered them, and prevailed against them, so that they fled out of that house naked and wounded. (Acts 19:13-16 NKJV)

Before we go any further, I just have to say that anytime you go into a fight up seven to one and you get beat so badly that you and your crew run away naked and wounded, please know that you have received a beating for the ages.

So, what went wrong? Why the beating when it *seemed* like Sceva's sons were doing the right thing and saying the right words? Could it be they were faking it, just mimicking what they heard someone else say?

In his book, *Operating in the Courts of Heaven*, Robert Henderson sheds some light on what happened. He says, "We cannot fake the spirit realm out. If we haven't been given the jurisdiction from Heaven to operate there, the spirit realm and its forces know it and will exploit it."[1]

So, what he is saying is the spirit realm can see a fake coming a mile away. "We exorcise you by the Jesus whom Paul preaches." In other words, Sceva's sons said to the evil spirit, "We exorcise you by the Jesus who some other guy has a relationship with, but we do not have a relationship with Him; we're just acting like we do." Now tell me, how much confidence would you have in a person who would say or even think this? I would assume not much.

Even though these men were sons of the chief priest, I believe it's safe to say they were not men who had a relationship with Jesus. They had heard about Jesus, but they had not permitted their lives to be touched and empowered by Him. The truth is they had no power, only presumption.

In Australia there is a bird known for its ability to mimic just about any sound it hears. This bird's ability to reproduce sounds like a human's voice or a ringing cell phone is uncanny. Its impersonation of a chainsaw and a car alarm is deceptively accurate. But even at that, this bird doesn't have the power to cut down trees or scare a thief away. It can only imitate the real thing. And, ironically, this bird is called a lyrebird (pronounced: liar-bird).

Just like the lyrebird, Sceva's sons were men mimicking what they heard. They used Jesus' name but had no power or authority to perform any act of deliverance. They sounded like the real thing, but they were not. They were men who faked their identity and relationship to Christ. Like their father Satan, they were proven to be *liar birds* – imposters without power.

God doesn't want the devil deceiving you, and He certainly doesn't want you deceiving yourself. I'll emphasize it again—it's important to be a tree rooted in the soil of God's Word and not Satan's. Why? Because of the fruit you will bear. In Matthew 7:15-20, Jesus warns:

"Beware of false prophets, who come to you in sheep's clothing, but inwardly they are ravenous wolves. You will know them by their fruits. Do men gather grapes from thornbushes or figs from thistles? Even so, every good tree bears good fruit, but a bad tree bears bad fruit. A good tree cannot bear bad fruit, nor can a bad tree bear good fruit. Every tree that does not bear good fruit is cut down and thrown into the fire. Therefore by their fruits you will know them.'" (Matthew 7:15-20 NKJV)

Jesus is saying don't be a liar bird, appearing as one thing when you are really something else. But, be assured, the fruit your actions produce will reveal your true identity.

Self-deception is one tactic the devil uses to try and render us ineffective. But too bad for him because we are here to be both effective and dangerous daughters of God. This means we take the offensive to protect our identities against self-deception, and we do that by guarding our hearts. In fact, the wisest man to ever live, King Solomon, admonishes us to guard our hearts, "So above all, guard the affections of your heart, for they affect all that you are. Pay attention to the welfare of your innermost being, for from there flows the wellspring of life" (Proverbs 4:23 TPT).

Jesus is the perfect example of someone who guarded His heart. As a result, He did not fall into self-deception or self-denial. He remained true to His identity and, in so doing, He remained true to His destiny. We can learn a lot from Jesus, and we will a little later in this chapter and the next.

Seeds of Doubt Planted in the Garden

Adam and Eve enjoyed spending time with God in the Garden. Every day they waited with anticipation for Him to come walk and talk with them in the cool of the day. They loved hearing God's voice until one day another voice was heard in the Garden. This voice came to plant seeds into a different kind of soil. This voice came to plant seeds of doubt into the dirt made flesh — Adam and Eve. And he, the devil, did it with a single question:

"Did God really say, 'You must not eat from any tree in the garden?'"
(Genesis 3:1b NIV)

I wish you could see my face right now because that question literally gets under my skin. It has "I'm being messy" written all over it. You can see it, right? There was no good morning, good day or hey y'all offered. Just doubt disguised as an innocent conversation.

God had communicated to Adam, who shared it with Eve, that they could eat of every tree in the Garden except one, the tree of the knowledge of good and evil. But notice how Satan twists his words to create a natural desire in Adam and Eve to correct his erroneous statement. Look at the question again. He's asking if God told them they're not to eat from *any* tree in the Garden. Do you think he already knew the answer? Of course he did.

But that's the nature of a serpent — to twist and turn things to get you to second guess the truth you've been told. And he's slick about it. Depending on the translation of the Bible you're reading, Satan is described as crafty, cunning, shrewd, clever, subtle, skilled in deceit.

Imagine that.

Since the beginning of mankind, Satan has been trying to get us to waiver in our belief of not only what God said, but in God Himself. If we don't fully trust what God says, then how confident can we be in what He says about us? And that, my friend, is the devil's end game.

In his book, *Restored*, Neil T. Anderson writes, "The power of Satan is in the lie, and the battle is for the mind. If he is able to deceive Christians into believing a lie, they will be spiritually impotent. He can't do anything about our identity and position in Christ, but if he can get us to believe it is not true, we will live as though it isn't. When the lies are exposed, Satan's power over the believer is broken.²"

In other words, who God created us to be in Christ Jesus never changes. It is settled. Believing the lies of Satan uproots us and places us in soil God never intended us to grow in. Let's dive deeper to see how this happened to Adam and Eve. Genesis 3:1-9 paints the picture well.

Now the serpent was more cunning than any beast of the field which the LORD God had made. And he said to the woman, "Has God indeed said, 'You shall not eat of every tree of the garden?'"

And the woman said to the serpent, "We may eat the fruit of the trees of the garden; but of the fruit of the tree which *is* in the midst of the garden, God has said, 'You shall not eat it, nor shall you touch it, lest you die.'"

Then the serpent said to the woman, "You will not surely die. For God knows that in the day you eat of it your eyes will be opened, and you will be like God, knowing good and evil."

So when the woman saw that the tree *was* good for food, that it *was* pleasant to the eyes, and a tree desirable to make *one* wise, she took of its fruit and ate. She also gave to her husband with her, and he ate. Then the eyes of both of them were opened, and they knew that they *were* naked; and they sewed fig leaves together and made themselves coverings.

And they heard the sound of the LORD God walking in the garden in the cool of the day, and Adam and his wife hid themselves from the presence of the LORD God among the trees of the garden.

Then the LORD God called to Adam and said to him, "Where are you?" (Genesis 3:1-9 NKJV)

I've read these verses many times in my life, but now, when I view them through the lens of identity, I see things much differently. God's question breaks my heart because I sense His heart is broken.

Where are you? You're no longer where I planted you.

Where are you? I'd like to walk with you in the Garden.

Where are you? I desire your presence.

Where are you? I don't like this separation between us.

Where are you? Are you lost?

I remember a time when a friend and I went to the mall to do some shopping. We were in a large department store when I heard a man's voice cry out over and over again the name of his child. I could hear the desperation in his voice and when I looked into his eyes, I could see the anguish. Even now it brings tears to my eyes thinking about it. I joined in on the search, and after a minute or two the father found his daughter hiding, playing under a clothes rack. She had quietly walked away from her father, unaware of the potential danger she put herself in. But her dad was determined to find her, and when he did, the joy and relief on his face, and I'm sure in his heart, were undeniable. His daughter was lost but was found and restored to him.

When Adam and Eve ate the fruit from the tree of the knowledge of good and evil, they walked away from God. At that moment, they were lost to Him, and a wall of separation was erected between them and God. Between us and God. But it wouldn't always be that way.

Have you ever listened to the song, "Reckless Love"? It's written and sung by Cory Asbury with Bethel Music. It

BUT WHO ARE YOU?

beautifully expresses the intensity of God's desire to restore us as His children.

There's no shadow You won't light up, mountain You won't climb up, coming after me. There's no wall You won't kick down, lie You won't tear down, coming after me.[3]

God had a plan to restore us back to Himself. His plan was intense, and some may even call it radical, but He sent His Son, Jesus, as a ransom for us all. God's love, His compassion, stopped at nothing to save us. Jesus came willingly, all the while knowing He would suffer and die in our place. And by doing so, He defeated the power of separation and sin the devil so slyly introduced in the Garden.

Into the Wild

At the cross was not the only time Jesus defeated Satan. There was another time — in the wilderness where the two came face to face. The wilderness can be described as an uncultivated, uninhabited region. It was the proving ground for Jesus just before He stepped into His ministry and true identity. What LoDebar, a place of barrenness, was to Mephibosheth, the wilderness was to Jesus. The difference between the two was that Mephibosheth was taken to LoDebar to hide. Jesus, on the other hand, was led into the wilderness to ultimately be revealed as the Christ, the Anointed One, the Son of the living God who would take away the sin of the world. Here's what the Bible says about Jesus' wilderness experience.

Then Jesus, being filled with the Holy Spirit, returned from the Jordan and was led by the Spirit into the wilderness, being tempted for forty days by the devil. And in those days He ate nothing, and afterward, when they had ended, He was hungry.

And the devil said to Him, "If You are the Son of God, command this stone to become bread."

But Jesus answered him, saying, "It is written, 'Man shall not live by bread alone, but by every word of God.'"

Then the devil, taking Him up on a high mountain, showed Him all the kingdoms of the world in a moment of time. And the devil said to Him, "All this authority I will give You, and their glory; for this has been delivered to me, and I give it to whomever I wish. Therefore, if You will worship before me, all will be Yours."

And Jesus answered and said to him, "Get behind Me, Satan! For it is written, 'You shall worship the LORD your God, and Him only you shall serve.'"

Then he brought Him to Jerusalem, set Him on the pinnacle of the temple, and said to Him, "If You are the Son of God, throw Yourself down from here. For it is written: 'He shall give His angels charge over you, To keep you,' and, 'In their hands they shall bear you up, Lest you dash your foot against a stone.'"

And Jesus answered and said to him, "It has been said, 'You shall not tempt the LORD your God.'" (Luke 4:1-12 NKJV)

The verses you just read are packed full of vital intel that shows the roundabout way Satan tried to get Jesus to forfeit His identity by submitting to his directives. If Jesus had listened to the devil, He would have surrendered His purpose and identity. He would have surrendered us.

Thankfully, Jesus knew who He was. He knew His identity and the inheritance, you and me, attached to it. Overcoming the temptations that day was not just a victory for Jesus, but one for us as well. Let's take a closer look at each temptation.

Temptation One

And the devil said to Him, "If You are the Son of God, command this stone to become bread." But Jesus answered him, saying, "It is written, 'Man shall not live by bread alone, but by every word of God.'" (Luke 4:3-4 NKJV)

"If You are the Son of God." I mean, what is this? It's Satan up to his old tricks again. Like with Adam and Eve in the Garden, he is attempting to create doubt and confusion in Jesus' mind about what God said to Him and about Him. One very important thing God said about Jesus was: **"You are My beloved Son; in You I am well pleased"** (Luke 3:22b NKJV). So much, as we will see in the next chapter, hinges on this declaration.

If Jesus would have complied with Satan's command and turned the stone into bread, then Jesus would have subjected Himself to Satan and put Himself under his authority.

The whole thing, what Satan was attempting to do, is rather silly when you think about it. He wanted Jesus, the Chief Cornerstone (Isaiah 28:16, Ephesians 2:20 NKJV), to take a stone and turn it into bread, something Jesus had already described Himself to be.

Then Jesus said to them, "Most assuredly, I say to you, Moses did not give you the bread from heaven, but My Father gives you the true bread from heaven. For the bread of God is He who comes down from heaven and gives life to the world."

Then they said to Him, "Lord, give us this bread always."

And Jesus said to them, "I am the bread of life. He who comes to Me shall never hunger, and he who believes in Me shall never thirst." (John 6:32-35 NKJV)

Satan quite often operates in the arena of quick fixes and temporary solutions. Bread to feed the stomach is a temporal thing. You'll be hungry again within hours of eating it. Not so with Jesus, the bread of life. Feasting on Him takes away soul hunger for a lifetime...actually, eternity.

I love that Jesus told Satan that man was to live by every word spoken by God for one simple fact: **Jesus is the Word!**

In the beginning was the Word, and the Word was with God, and the Word was God. He was with God in the beginning. Through him all things were made; without him nothing was made that has been made. In him was life, and that life was the light of all mankind. The light shines in the darkness, and the darkness has not overcome it. (John 1:1-5 NIV)

Satan came for Jesus, but Jesus was ready for him. Jesus basically told Satan, "If I understand you correctly, you want Me (Jesus) to make Me (Bread of Life) out of Me (Chief Cornerstone). I know you're talking about bread that fills the stomach, but I'm talking about bread that gives life and fills the soul. All should know that mankind is not to live by only eating temporal bread, but by feasting on every Word of God. Oh, and by the way, I am that Word."

Don't you just love it!?

Temptation Two

Then the devil, taking Him up on a high mountain, showed Him all the kingdoms of the world in a moment of time. And the devil said to Him, "All this authority I will give You, and their glory; for this has been delivered to me, and I give it to whomever I wish. Therefore, if You will worship before me, all will be Yours." And Jesus answered and said to him, "Get behind Me, Satan! For it is written, 'You shall worship the LORD your God, and Him only you shall serve.'" (Luke 4:5-8 NKJV)

There are a number of truths presented in this chapter. And one that I hope you've caught on to by now is that the devil is a master of deception. Constantly putting forth false narratives, his lies are designed to steal your identity, abolish your authority, and rob you of your inheritance. But knowing and living by the truth puts a major wrench in Satan's plans for off-coursing and even destroying your life. Jesus Himself said, "'If you hold to my teaching, you are really my disciples. Then you will know the truth, and the truth will set you free'" (John 8:31b-32 NIV).

Being a devoted reader of the Scriptures and a person of prayer, Jesus knew what the Word and the Father said about Him. Knowing He was the Son of God made resisting Satan's temptations easier to endure and overcome. The same can be true for us too as God's daughters. The key is knowing the Word, believing the Word, and living by the Word. There's no better example Jesus could have given us to overcome Satan than with the Word.

Showing Jesus all the kingdoms of the world and offering to give Him their authority and glory was one of the most ridiculous proposals Satan could have made. Who in their right mind, desiring something from someone, would offer to give them something they already owned? That's like someone showing you all the clothes in your closet and saying to you, "All these pants, dresses, shirts, and shoes that you own I will give you if you will only bow down and worship me."

And Satan knew full-well who Jesus was. Before he was cast out of heaven, the two were in glory together. So, the question begs to be asked: how are you going to offer earthly glory to Jesus, who, according to 1 Corinthians 2:8, is the Lord of glory, and who came from glory? There's no comparison.

Satan operates in the realm of the fast and temporal. He entices by making quick, short-term gains appear more appealing than they are. In reality, it's all a guise to destroy your identity, and thereby your purpose and soul.

Jesus Himself said, "'For what profit is it to a man if he gains the whole world, and loses his own soul? Or what will a man give in exchange for his soul?'" (Matthew 16:26 NKJV). Now, those are words to make you stop and think. Is there anything you are willing to exchange your soul for? Think about that for a moment.

When Jesus heard Satan's proposal, He didn't respond with shouting or physical force to thwart Satan's temptation. He used the living Word. **"For it is written, 'You shall worship the LORD your God, and Him only you shall serve'"** (Luke 4:8 NKJV).

Perhaps Jesus pulled from 1 Samuel 7:3-4, Joshua 22:5, or the Scripture below:

"'And if you will indeed obey my commandments that I command you today, to love the LORD your God, and to serve him with all your heart and with all your soul, he will give the rain for your land in its season, the early rain and the later rain, that you may gather in your grain and your wine and your oil. And he will give grass in your fields for your livestock, and you shall eat and be full. Take care lest your heart be deceived, and you turn aside and serve other gods and worship them; then the anger of the LORD will be kindled against you, and he will shut up the heavens, so that there will be no rain, and the land will yield no fruit, and you will perish quickly off the good land that the LORD is giving you.'" (Deuteronomy 11:13-17 ESV)

I bet Satan was hoping Jesus wasn't aware of that particular Scripture passage or any others similar to it. How much you want to bet he hopes you're not aware either. Well, too late!

Temptation Three

Then he brought Him to Jerusalem, set Him on the pinnacle of the temple, and said to Him, "If You are the Son of God, throw Yourself down from here. For it is written: 'He shall give His angels charge over you, To keep you,' and, 'In their hands they shall bear you up, Lest you dash your foot against a stone.'" And Jesus answered and said to him, "It has been said, 'You shall not tempt the LORD your God.'" (Luke 4:9-12 NKJV)

The master manipulator was at it again, wanting Jesus to prove He was God's Son. This time he attempted to make a wrong thing seem right by mimicking Jesus in using Scripture. But Jesus wasn't falling for it, nor was He going to fall from the top of any temple. The only one who fell was Satan, and to this day he's seeking to ascend to a place and position he can never occupy. He will never be like the Most High

God, and he will never sit on or above His throne. The reality is that he was brought down low and will be brought down lower still. Every time he attacks your identity and destiny, remind him what the Bible says about his identity and destiny. Girl, put the Word on him with this Scripture passage from Isaiah:

"How you are fallen from heaven, O Lucifer, son of the morning! How you are cut down to the ground, You who weakened the nations! For you have said in your heart: 'I will ascend into heaven, I will exalt my throne above the stars of God; I will also sit on the mount of the congregation on the farthest sides of the north; I will ascend above the heights of the clouds, I will be like the Most High.' Yet you shall be brought down to Sheol, To the lowest depths of the Pit." (Isaiah 14:12-15 NKJV)

Jesus, knowing that He was in the Father and the Father was in Him (John 14:9-11) and that He and God are one (John 10:30), silenced Satan's third temptation with these words:

"You shall not tempt, <u>the LORD your God.</u>"

Jesus' response was brilliant. If Satan was asking, "But who are You?," he got the answer of a lifetime — **the LORD your God.** Yes, even Jesus' enemies will one day, at the mention of His name, bow their knees and confess that Jesus is Lord (Philippians 2:10-11).

On to Revelation

Whew! Our reconnaissance mission dug up a lot of intel on our enemy, did it not? We now have a better understanding of Satan — who he is, how he operates, and how he can be defeated. Let's recap what we've learned.

The chapter opened with the question, *Who are you?* To know the answer to this question takes knowing God's Word. It's a powerful weapon in dispelling the lies of Satan. Always remember, it's the truth of God's Word that will guard your heart and mind.

The seven sons of Sceva showed us how our enemy can manipulate us to the point of self-deception, making a fool of anyone who dares to be an imposter without power. Planting seeds of doubt about our true identity is yet another one of Satan's tactics. In the Garden of Eden he lied to Adam and Eve, and when they acted on those lies, they, and us, became separated from God. But God's gracious plan has always been to restore us through the death and resurrection of His Son, Jesus Christ.

And it was Jesus who showed us how to stop boxing the air and land some punches by how He handled Satan's temptations. Jesus' weapon was God's Word. It's in how He wielded the Word that we learn how to fight like Him. Jesus showed us we must know the Word, believe the Word, and live by the Word if we are to know who we are. The revelation of who Jesus is is the key to unlocking and revealing our identities and so much more.

CHAPTER 5

This Is Who I Am

"And now I'm going to tell you who you are, really are."
—Matthew 16:18a (MSG)

"I AM THIS."

As I watched Marvel's *Avengers: Endgame* I was surprised by how these words impacted me. Traveling back in time, Nebula from the past concedes her identity to be that of a deceitful, broken, anger-filled murderer. I don't believe for a minute it was who she wanted to be, but it was what life's circumstances made her.

It seemed Nebula hated everybody and everything. She destroyed and pillaged just like her father, Thanos, taught her to. He did it for power. She did it hoping to gain his approval. The sad thing is she never received it.

In reality, approval and acceptance were foreign to Nebula because in her world she only knew rejection. Anything her father deemed inferior about her he replaced with mechanized, inanimate parts until she became cold and unfeeling just like them. But can you blame her? She, like many women, found a way to deaden the pain inside her heart and silence the thoughts inside her head that constantly told her she was not enough.

What a terrible existence. Nebula lost her identity because Thanos' way of life became her way of life. His way of thinking became her way of thinking until his thoughts about who she was overshadowed her own. Could this be your reality too? If it is, what are you prepared to do about it? I say we put into practice the skills we learned in the previous chapter. We *fight like Jesus* to defeat Thanos.

Defeating Thanos is all about defeating the devil and recovering all that he took from us. Did you know the Bible (Proverbs 6:31) says that when a thief is caught, he must pay back seven times what he took, even if it cost him all the wealth of his house? So you know what you gotta do, right? Make it your mission to partner with God to reclaim your identity and bankrupt the devil in the process.

Cut My Check and Pay Me

In Chapter 1, I shared with you how an ill-gotten kiss from a guy who had a girlfriend became the gateway to my being the supporting actress instead of the leading lady in relationships. My settling on second became a cycle that was difficult for me to break. Highlight these next four words: **Never settle on second**.

Isn't it interesting that while I was writing this book Satan was up to his old tricks by putting an old temptation in front of me? We'll call him "Kryptonite."

Do you know what kryptonite is? Metaphorically speaking, it's anything that robs you of your strength or weakens you in some capacity, as the element (kryptonite) did to comic book superhero, Superman.

Kryptonite was a former boyfriend. I was his girlfriend at one point in time and the alternate chick at others. I guess I should not have been surprised how, some 30+ years later, he still saw me as that "supporting actress." Even if he didn't consciously think of it that way, that was the reality of it.

I had heard rumors Kryptonite had gotten married, but no one really knew for sure because he didn't tell family or friends, and I had not seen or talked with him in years. However, in 2020 he came by for a visit and was the perfect gentleman. Oh, yes– I did check for a wedding band or the indentation of one. Didn't see either, but why didn't I just flat-out ask? Avoidance. If the rumors were true I knew I would have to completely sever ties, and I didn't like the finality of that. I believe it's called Hang-on-to-a-pipe-dream-itis. However, in more scholarly circles, it's known as dysfunction.

In 2022, I received a text message out of the blue from Kryptonite asking if he could stay at my house while attending an event in town. Finally, tired of stringing my own self along, I asked about his marital status.

"Did you go and get married on me?" I asked, trying to keep it light.

"I gave it a shot," was his reply.

I didn't take it further than that. My original interpretation of his response was he tried marriage, but it didn't work out. Later that evening God put it on my heart to read his response again.

Oh, that was crafty. On second look, I realized "I gave it a shot," could easily mean either it did or did not work out. The following day I just flat out asked, "Were or are you married? Yes or no?" The text back to me read, "Yes, I was and I still am."

I literally wanted to go off. I thought, "What kind of woman does he think I am to have a married man staying in my house? But God didn't permit me to go off on him. Instead, He directed me to go in on myself.

Did you put yourself in the position of being seen as a "supporting actress"?

Yes.

Was there a time when you were ok with settling for second?

Yes.

Did you think in your youth it was all about the present fun and not about the future consequences?

Yes.

Was it worth it?

No.

I couldn't be angry with Kryptonite or anyone else because I permitted it. I always had a choice and time, and again I chose poorly. That's what not knowing your identity will do to you. You'll let circumstances and others define you even if you see yourself differently. Are you tracking with me?

But that's who I was. It's not who I am today. The woman I am today is the woman who responded back with a prayerful heart, desiring not to tear down, but to build up (even while I was still feeling some kind of way about the situation). Here's how God directed me to respond:

"It impacts a woman's self-esteem when she is hidden. Honor your wife and proudly let people know who she is.

"There's no way I can allow a married man to stay at my home. It would diminish my worth and integrity to do so. That's something I can't do and you can't either. I wish you the very best in life."

And that ended our communication.

But that's not the end of the story. There was one more thing that needed to happen and that was removing his number from my phone. I have to tell you I struggled with it.

I shared the entire experience with Ushirika Johnson, a dear friend. She listened as a friend, but as a licensed counselor, she encouraged me to sit with and process why I was struggling to delete the number. A couple of days passed, and I eventually came up with "He's married and he doesn't need the potential drama." But then my thinking shifted. Why was I concerned more about him than myself? As I lay on my bed that night, I realized I had not completely severed myself from that "settling for second" mentality.

The next morning the first thing I did was delete the phone number. And guess what happened? The world kept right on spinning. It was not the end of the world but the beginning of a brand new one.

The devil wanted to keep me in the chains of my past, that old identity, but I counter-punched his punch and hit him with the Word. I said in essence, "It is written, 'If the Son sets me free, **I am free** indeed'" (John 8:36).

What made the difference? Studying God's Word to write this book built me up and made me stronger, proving Jesus' words in 2 Corinthians 12:9 to be true, "'My grace is sufficient for you, for My strength is made perfect in weakness.'"

Is God stronger than your kryptonite? He absolutely is. So go ahead and use His Word to bankrupt the devil. And then tell that thief and robber of identities to pay up and cut you your check.

Identity Lost. Identity Found.

In many ways, Whitney's college experience was like most students, days of classes and nights of sporting events and parties. But then some things were different. For Whitney, one thing in particular.

Whitney was intently pursued by one of the college's star basketball players. Was it for friendship or something else? Whitney wasn't sure. Something just didn't sit right with her about it, though. To others it seemed innocent enough, but as things turned out it wasn't.

While in her dorm room by herself, there came an unexpected knock at the door. Whitney opened it, and there stood the basketball player. A step over the threshold and a locked door later, Whitney was taken advantage of by a star player of the women's basketball team.

What followed were years of living a compromised lifestyle, as Satan tried to get Whitney to deny who God created her to be. But there were two things he didn't count on. One was Whitney's strong sense of self, and the other was God's pursuit of Whitney being greater than that of the basketball player's. Below Whitney shares her story:

I grew up in a seventh-generation Christian home, but even at that, my family still had its struggles. As I was finding my identity, deaths, disappointments, divisions, and caretaker responsibilities consumed my high school years, but somehow I still found time to play sports.

When I entered college, I was like, this is my time. I'm away from everything, so I'm just going to live the college life. I just started partying, frat parties, you name it, just living the college life.

A few weeks in, I received an instant message from a star basketball player that said, "Hey, I would love to hang out sometime." For some reason, I didn't feel at peace with it. I told my mom about the message, and she was like, "Whitney, it's fine. You're in college, make friends."

I let the matter go, but one night there was a knock at my dorm room door and it was that basketball player. She came into my room, closed the door, locked it, and took full advantage of me.

Growing up we're taught the moral thing to do if a guy comes on to you, but not what to do if it's someone of the same sex. And so I just remember how that night, she took my phone, called herself so she would have my phone number, and then walked out of the room.

It was at that point I started living multiple lives. So I had my frat party life, where I would go hang out with my girls and we'd hang out with the frat boys. And I was talking to some guys. And then I joined a business fraternity, and I was the vice president of that, so I had my business life. But then I had this confused side of life, and because of the bashing I witnessed of others, the last thing I was going to do was run back home and say, "Hey, I'm confused." I just resolved I would figure things out on my own.

I was fortunate throughout my time in college to have a mom and grandmas who were praying me into a real relationship with Christ. The truth is I knew about Jesus, but I didn't know Jesus.

I started hanging out with a lot of the girls who called themselves gay and lesbian and things like that, but they never forced me to call myself that. They accepted who I was and whoever I wanted to be with. The enemy really used this. I started to agree with the notion you are what happened to you. So I walked in that lifestyle for a while and was in a relationship with a girl for a couple of years.

Then one day I was invited to Campus Outreach by one of my friends that I had been partying with. She had given her life to Christ and just kept inviting me. Eventually, I did agree to go because I saw the change in her. It was a Passion Conference held in Atlanta, Georgia. It was there that I gave my life to Christ. It was there that I realized the difference between religion and relationship, and the choice was on the table. Do you want to have a relationship with Christ? And I just broke. I remember just weeping and just being like, "Lord, if you want to take me where I am, take me."

I returned to college and broke up with my girlfriend. I told her that I was choosing a relationship with Jesus over a relationship with her.

I believe until you know whose you are, you will never truly know who you are. And what I mean by this is, it doesn't really matter what one's identity may be attached to. It could be your sexuality. It could be your job. It could be playing sports. It could be being a parent. Whatever it may be, everyone is in an identity crisis until they find their primary identity in Christ Jesus. Until you understand the character of who Jesus is and who you are in Him, you're experiencing an identity crisis, and you don't even know it. So until you go from the identity crisis to identity in Christ, it's all skewed.

Homosexuality is a sensitive topic, to be sure, but it's one that should not be swept under the rug. I'm grateful to Whitney for her courage and candor in sharing her story. It's because of her experience in the lifestyle that I felt she was the perfect person to speak to it. Personally, I do want to say to people reading this book who are living a homosexual lifestyle that you, as a human being, are God's workmanship (Ephesians 2:10) made in His image. But, please know that Jesus did not die on a cross to save someone's sexual orientation. That's not your identity. He died to save those who would one day become children of God.

If you are thinking about leaving the homosexual lifestyle and would like more information to learn how you can, visit https://www.freedomtomarch.com. You can also send an email to freedomlife4him@gmail.com to receive encouraging support to help you in your journey.

When Present Meets Past

The past reminds us of what was. It can offer great memories and joy as well as sadness and regret. If the latter, wouldn't it be nice to travel back in time to change things? Present-day Nebula (I bet you thought I forgot about her) got the opportunity to do it. By this time in the story she had transformed into a likable character who was on the side of good and fighting for it. She steps into a scenario where she comes face to face with her former self. Want to know what she was doing? What she had always done. Holding a weapon on someone ready to kill them. That's when present-day Nebula began to speak to her past self.

"You don't have to do this," Nebula tells her former self.

"I am this," was the response.

"You can change."

With heartbreaking anguish on her face, she replies, "He [Thanos] won't let me."

She then turns her weapon on Gamora, her sister, the one she lived in the shadow of. She points to shoot. A shot rings out, and it's Nebula (past) who goes down as present-day Nebula shoots her old identity and renders her past dead. In so doing, she freed herself to be exactly who she was created to be and not what another person or circumstance made her.

I Was. I Am.

Although Nebula's story is fiction, I believe it is based on reality for a lot of women reading this book, and you may be one of them. Whitney and I are two others. How Nebula finished figuratively paints the picture of what we need to do to render our pasts dead, just like these women in the Bible:

Sarah, the wife of Abraham, was childless, but God promised they would have a son. At the age of 90 Sarah gave birth to Isaac (Genesis 17:15-17; 18:10-14; 21:1-3). Sarah could tell the world, "I was barren, but now **I am fruitful. I am the mother of kings. I am the mother of nations.**"

Rahab traded sex for money. She was a prostitute. But it was through her wisdom and shrewdness in hiding two Israeli spies that her entire family was saved. They were protected and led out of Jericho when Israel later attacked the city. Rahab became the wife of Salmon, an Israelite, and they had a son named Boaz. She became the great, great grandmother to King David and is included in the lineage of Jesus (Joshua 2; 6:17-18, 22-25; Matthew 1:5).

Rahab could tell you, "I was a prostitute, but today **I am a virtuous woman. I am accepted into God's family.**"

Ruth forsook her people and culture to follow her mother-in-law, Naomi, back to Bethlehem. Both women's husbands had died in Moab, leaving them widows. Ruth gleaned wheat and barley from a field so both she and Naomi could eat. Turns out the field belonged to none other than Boaz, Rahab and Salmon's son. He was a close family relative who could pay the price necessary to purchase the land that once belonged to Naomi's husband and two sons. Naomi instructed Ruth on what to do and Boaz picked it up from there until he had redeemed the land and made Ruth his wife (Ruth 1-4). If you could talk with Ruth today, she would tell you, "I was a widow in a foreign land without the covering of a husband, but today **I am married. I am covered. I am protected. I am redeemed.**"

Then there's **Mary Magdalene** who was demon-possessed, but because of Christ's intervention in her life she was able to testify, "**I am delivered**" (Matthew 16:9).

There is the **unnamed woman** who had been bleeding for twelve years. She was considered unclean and an outcast among her people. She spent her livelihood on doctors, but they were not able to help her. But one day Jesus drew near, and in faith she pressed through the crowd believing if she could somehow touch Him, she would be healed. She reached out and managed to touch the hem of His garment. However, it was her faith that touched Jesus and released the power she needed to be made whole again. Jesus said to her,

"Daughter, be of good cheer; your faith has made you well. Go in peace." This woman was sick, unclean, and untouchable. But because of her encounter with Jesus, she would tell you, "**I am healed. I am clean. I am touchable**" (Luke 8:43-48).

As Jesus taught in the temple a group of scribes and Pharisees brought a **woman caught in adultery** before Him. These men wanted her condemned and stoned to death for her sin. Jesus dispersed her accusers with one simple statement, "Let any one of you who is without sin be the first to throw a stone at her." The men left one by one until it was only Jesus and the woman left in the temple. No one was without sin and no one could condemn her. Jesus, Himself, did not condemn her. He told her to "...go, and sin no more." Until she met Jesus she was subject to being condemned and dying. After meeting Jesus she could tell anyone in her town, "**I am forgiven**" (John 8:1-11).

These women's lives changed when they encountered God, either through His favor or His Son. They went from their old "I was" to their new "I am" when they came in contact with God, the original I AM (read Exodus 3:13-14).

In Conclusion

As this chapter and book come to a close, let's recap what we learned about our identities.

In Chapter 1 we learned God knows everything about us because He created us, and like any good father would about his children, He declares we are His. The various titles and roles we have (i.e. mother, wife, child, aunt, sister, employee, etc.) do not make up our identities. They are components of our identities, not the core. Remove the man-made titles and roles and what remains is who God created you and me to be. We are His daughters, and it's from this truth we begin to grow in the knowledge of who we are.

In Chapter 2 we discovered a just and righteous King will love and acknowledge us despite the reason or condition of our lameness. He will search for us when we have fallen and hidden ourselves. He will call us out of dead and barren places and restore to us all we have lost, and He will bless and accept us as one of His children, making room for us to always have a seat at His table. Lameness and imperfection don't cause God to reject us. They stir up His desire to restore us and make us whole as He always intended.

Chapter 3 showed us the power and importance of a name. Jacob, also known as Israel, changed his son's name to Benjamin (son of my right hand) when, at the point of death, his wife Rachel named him Ben-Oni (son of my sorrow). Living with the name the Father gives places us under His covering and Lordship, and reinforces who we are and who we belong to. This helps us better understand the powers and weight given to the name of Jesus. It is His name that is above every name and it is His name that has the power to save, redeem, and reconcile us back to God.

In Chapter 4 we pulled the mask off the devil and exposed the tactics he uses to keep us distracted and distanced from knowing and walking in our true identity. His temptation of the Savior schooled us in the fine art of how to fight like Jesus for our identities. There was nothing Jesus needed to do or prove to Satan. What Satan thought didn't matter. What God thought did. Jesus was confident in His relationship with the Father. He was the Son of God, and it was settled, just like it is for us as God's daughters. No argument was needed. The Word spoken and applied proved more than enough to shut the mouth of Satan.

And now, here we are in the fifth and final chapter. For me, it has been a journey of profound vulnerability, discovery, and revelation. A bit uncomfortable, but well worth the effort to be set free from my old identity to embrace my new identity as a child of God.

I started this book with one question on my mind: Who am I? Quite frankly, I didn't know. I was going on how I felt and what others said. I did not take the time to study what God said about me and see it through to the end until now, and all I can say is, "WOW!" I searched for God, and I found Him and who I am in Him, proving Jeremiah 29:13 true, "And you will seek Me and find Me, when you search for Me with all your heart" (NKJV).

Search for Him, my sister. Search for who you are in Him and don't relent until you confidently know who you are based on His Word. So go ahead and call Him. He is waiting to reveal to you the depths and purpose of your identity. He bids you to call to Him, "'Call to Me, and I will answer you, and show you great and mighty things, which you do not know'" (Jeremiah 33:3 NKJV).

And yet, there is more to be revealed.

The Ultimate Revelation

Jesus once asked His disciples, "'Who do people say that I am?' They responded telling Him, 'Some say John the Baptist, Elijah, Jeremiah or one of the other prophets.' He then asked, 'Who do you say I am?' and one of the disciples, Simon Peter to be exact, gave the following answer: **You're the Christ, the Messiah, the Son of the living God'**" (read Matthew 16:13-16).

Jesus came back, " 'God bless you, Simon, son of Jonah! You didn't get that answer out of books or from teachers. My Father in heaven, God himself, let you in on this secret of who I really am. **And now I'm going to tell you who you are, really are.** You are Peter, a rock. This is the rock on which I will put together my church, a church so expansive with energy that not even the gates of hell will be able to keep it out'" (Matthew 16:17-18 MSG).

We can glean so much insight from the two paragraphs above:

- Those who did not know Jesus personally only assumed who He might be.

- Who Jesus was was revealed to someone who walked closely with Him and had a relationship with Him.

- It was the revelation of who Jesus was _first_ that led to Peter discovering who he really was.

- The very gates of hell cannot, nor will they ever, prevail against the power and authority of the revealed Christ.

Jesus goes on to tell Peter, "And I will give you the keys of the kingdom of heaven, and whatever you bind on earth will be bound in heaven, and whatever you loose on earth will be loosed in heaven'" (Matthew 16:19 NKJV).

What's true for Peter is true for you and me. If we embrace our identities in Christ as children of God (read Galatians 3:26 and Romans 8:16-17) then we have access to and authority within His kingdom.

So now you know what the second book in this three-part series is going to be about. Yes, it's **_authority_**. And I hope you will join me on that journey of discovery as well.

Father,

Bless every woman who has read this book. Bless her as You bring her into alignment with her true identity. I pray with every word read and each page turned that her eyes were opened to the truth of who You called her to be. You called her out of darkness into Your marvelous light. She is Your daughter, and it is Christ who makes that possible. Your Word says in John 1:12, "But as many as received Him, to them He gave the right to become children of God." If my sister has not received Jesus Christ as her personal Lord and Savior, my prayer is that she does it right now by praying these words:

Father, I ask you to forgive me of my sins. I believe Jesus Christ is Your Son and that He died to cleanse me of my sins. I choose this day to make Him my Lord and Savior. Thank You for giving Jesus the power to lay down His life and to take it back up again. Because He lives, so do I as Your daughter. Thank you Father. I am eternally grateful. Amen.

Now, may the revelation of who Christ is and what He accomplished to set my sister free from the lies of a false identity be understood, graciously received, and powerfully lived to bring glory to Your name and restoration to the families all around the world. It is in the wonderful name of Jesus this prayer is offered.

Amen.

DISCUSSION QUESTIONS

Chapter 1

1. Re-read the first two paragraphs of chapter 1 and then answer the following questions: Would your heart melt with gladness or harden with resistance if God spoke those words to you? Why or why not?

2. Over the course of your life, what would you say has had the greatest impact on how you see yourself?

3. If God's word is not defining you, who or what is?

4. What lie has Satan told you about your identity?

5. In relation to your identity, how can you give God free rein to bury the past and resurrect the precious?

6. The author shared several stories (Kiss of Death/personal, You Are Free/butterfly, Thief in the Garden/Adam and Eve) in this chapter. Which of these stories resonated the most with you and why?

7. In what way did this chapter help you view your identity differently?

8. What resonated the most with you in this chapter? Why?

Chapter 2

1. Traumatic circumstances crippled Mephibosheth mentally and physically. He hid himself and his identity in Lo Debar, a barren land, where most would not suspect a member of the royal family to live. Mephibosheth became known as lame because of a fall that crippled him. How common is it today to equate someone by the "fall" he or she has taken?

2. Have you experienced a fall that left you with a label that represents the situation, but does not accurately reflect who you are? Do you still carry this identity? If so, what will it take to get rid of this false label?

3. Satan is all about planting seeds of doubt in our minds regarding our identities? Why do you think that is?

4. What seed did he plant in Maggie's mind when she was just a child?

5. In Mephibosheth's and Maggie's stories, the King showed them kindness by restoring them to how He always saw them. How did King David restore Mephibosheth? How did the King restore Maggie?

6. Do you currently struggle with your identity in any way? If so, please share how.

7. Jesus asked the man at the pool of Bethesda if he wanted to be made well. If Jesus asked you this same question, what would be your response and why? (*Important Note: Faith is what Mephibosheth, Maggie, and the man at the pool of Bethesda demonstrated. They believed the word of the King.*)

8. What resonated the most with you in this chapter? Why?

Chapter 3

1. If Jacob/Israel did not change his son's name to Benjamin, how might constantly being called Ben-Oni (son of my sorrow) impact his life?

2. Do you think being named Benjamin (son of my right hand, strength, honor, authority) influenced his life in any way? Why, or why not?

3. What gives a name power?

4. Jacob lived up to the meaning of his name. He was a trickster and supplanter. But he received a new name after his encounter with God. God blessed him with the name, Israel (prevails with God), and with that new name came a new nature. What does this tell you about the power of a name?

5. There are names we're given at birth and names we're called later in life. Do you believe one carries more influence over a person's identity than the other? Explain your answer.

6. Why did the author believe it would have been a mistake to give the name Gimpy to her dog, Timmie? Does this make you more conscious of the names you speak over yourself and others?

7. Have you ever called yourself stupid when you did something silly, or called a bad driver an idiot? On the surface these labels may seem light and innocent but what does James 3:9-12 say?

8. The author stated that becoming a child of God is like being "reset to the original manufacturer's design and operating for the precise purpose for which the Creator intended. This is who you are. This is your identity." Do you agree or disagree with this statement? Why or why not.

9. What does it mean for you to know that, someday in Heaven, you will be given your real name by Jesus (Revelations 2:17)?

10. Identity thieves have been around for a long time. There's nothing new under the sun. The Chaldeans set out to change the culture of Daniel, Hananiah, Mishael, and Azariah by first changing their names and then their language, education, and even attempting to change their tastes in food (Daniel 1:3-7). What examples of this do you see in today's culture? What do you see as a solution to this identity theft?

11. What resonated the most with you in this chapter? Why?

Chapter 4

1. Our roles do not define our identities. When roles are removed, we get to the essence of who we are and who God made us to be. Do you agree with this statement? Why or why not?

2. God designed us to be His children and Jesus' sacrifice makes it possible. What action must a person take to be called a child of God (John 1:12; 3:16)?

3. Being a child of God is to have a personal relationship with Him through His Son, Jesus Christ. Only then can

we operate powerfully in Jesus' name and be about the Father's business. This understanding is something the seven sons of Sceva lacked and they paid dearly for it. Their assumption of having the power to exorcise demons was really self-deception. When it comes to your identity, why is self-deception dangerous?

4. What can a person do to avoid self-deception?

5. At every turn, Satan will try to get you to deny who you are or make you think you are someone God **never** said you were. What does Satan gain if he is successful in his deception? What is his end game?

6. Why is it important to know your enemy (Satan, the original identity thief) and his tactics?

7. Jesus proved being rooted in God's word and not in Satan's soil is the key to living victoriously as a child of God. Read Luke 4:1-12, and then answer the following question. What tactical strategies does Jesus demonstrate and teach us to use to defeat Satan's attacks against our identities?

8. What resonated the most with you in this chapter? Why?

Chapter 5

1. To reclaim her identity, Nebula had to overcome the lies her father ingrained into her thinking. We, on the other hand, must learn to defend ourselves from the destructive words the father of lies (John 8:44b) throws at us. What does Nebula's identity story teach you about your own story?

2. The author shared that she had been "settling for second" in her relationships. How might settling for second impact your identity?

3. Kryptonite is anything that robs you of your strength or weakens you in some capacity. What would you consider to be kryptonite to your identity?

4. In her Kryptonite story, the author wanted to go off, but God directed her to go in. She realized and had to acknowledge what she permitted. If God directed you to go in, what might you discover you permitted?

5. Whitney shared her powerful testimony of coming out of a homosexual lifestyle. Read the last paragraph of her story (pp. 75-76) and share with the group if you agree or disagree with her statement. Explain why or why not?

6. You read the "I Was-I Am" statements from women in the Bible: Sarah, Rahab, Ruth, Mary Magdalene, the woman with the issue of blood, and the woman caught in adultery. After reading this book, what might you say is your "I Was-I Am" statement?

7. The ultimate revelation to knowing and walking in our true identity only comes from knowing Christ and having a relationship with Him. Jesus did His part. Now it is up to you to do your part. What does that look like? (Hint: read Matthew 16:17-18).

8. What resonated the most with you in this chapter? Why?

9. What is your biggest takeaway from this book?

ABOUT THE AUTHOR

Alicia Terry is a truth seeker and her writing reflects it. She is a communications professional and master storyteller who uses her gifts of candor, transparency, and humor to inform, educate, and move people to action. Her heart's desire is to help people discover who they are in Christ and to courageously live from that identity and vantage point to honor God and build His kingdom.

Website: https://abovethefraypublishing.com

Instagram: https://instagram.com/AbovetheFrayPublishing

Pinterest: https://www.pinterest.com/AbovetheFrayPublishing

ENDNOTES

Chapter 1

1 https://www.merriam-webster.com/dictionary/enmity

Chapter 2

1Lo Debar: https://www.abarim-publications.com/Meaning/LoDebar.html

2Schatzmann, S. (B.A., M.Div., Ph.D.). (2002). "Note from John 5:2." *New Spirit-Filled Life Bible* (NKJV). Nashville, TN, Thomas Nelson. p. 1451.

Chapter 3

1Jimmy Evans – Overcoming Rejection – The Overcoming Life series, April 23, 2018, YouTube: https://www.youtube.com/watch?v=ACrPjqTxCkE.

Chapter 4

1Henderson, R. (2014). *Operating in the Courts of Heaven: Granting God the Legal Right to Fulfill His Passion and Answer Our Prayers*. Robert Henderson Ministries, p. 151.

2Anderson, N.T. (2007). *Experience Life with Jesus.* http://restored.pub/

[3] Asbury, C., Culver, C., & Jackson, R.(2017). Reckless Love [Lyrics]. Retrieved from https://www.youtube.com/watch?v=6xx0d3R2LoU

PERSONAL
NOTES

CHAPTER 1
You Are Mine

But now thus says the Lord, he who created you, O Jacob, he who formed you, O Israel: "Fear not, for I have redeemed you; I have called you by name, you are mine."

—Isaiah 43:1 (ESV)

_____

_____

_____

_____

_____

_____

_____

_____

_____

_____

CHAPTER 2
Not Forgotten

Now David said, "Is there still anyone who is left of the house of Saul, that I may show him kindness for Jonathan's sake?" ...And Ziba said to the king, "There is still a son of Jonathan who is lame in his feet."

—2 Samuel 9:1, 3b (NKJV)

_____

_____

_____

_____

_____

_____

_____

_____

_____

_____

_____

_____

CHAPTER 3
The Power of a Name

And so it was, as her soul was departing (for she died), that she called his name Ben-Oni; but his father called him Benjamin.

—Genesis 35:18 (NKJV)

_____

_____

_____

_____

_____

_____

_____

_____

_____

_____

_____

_____

_____

_____

_____

_____

_____

_____

_____

_____

_____

_____

_____

_____

_____

_____

_____

_____

_____

_____

_____

_____

CHAPTER 4
But Who Are You?

And the evil spirit answered and said, "Jesus I know, and Paul I know; but who are you?"

—Acts 19:15 (NKJV)

_____

_____

_____

_____

_____

_____

_____

_____

_____

_____

_____

_____

_____

CHAPTER 5

This Is Who I Am

"And now I'm going to tell you who you are, really are."
—*Matthew 16:18a (MSG)*

_____

_____

_____

_____

_____

_____

_____

_____

_____

_____

_____

_____